DUTCH OVEN

CAJUN AND CREOLE

BILL RYAN

GIBBS SMITH
TO ENRICH AND INSPIRE HUMANKIND

To my son Will; for joining scouts and allowing me to play along. As you made your way to becoming an Eagle Scout, I learned a new hobby of Dutch oven cooking. Mom and I are proud of you!

To Lake Bistineau State Park in Doyline, Louisana; for all the support provided for our monthly Dutch oven gatherings where many of these recipes were created, tested, and approved of to be good.

To Jeff and Stephine Jimes; Stephine for allowing Jeff to come outside and play, and Jeff, for all the conversations we have had while driving over 15,000 miles since 2007 to attend cook-offs, and for all the dishes we have dreamed up while on the road. Here's to many more miles and cook-offs, my friend.

To my best friend, lover, and wife Laura; thanks for letting me have fun with this, and for being honest and telling me to never cook a dish again and throw that recipe away. I fall in love with you all over again each day.

First Edition
16 15 14 13 12   5 4 3 2 1

Text © 2012 Bill Ryan
Photographs © 2012 Zac Williams

Published by
Gibbs Smith
P.O. Box 667
Layton, Utah 84041

1.800.835.4993 orders
www.gibbs-smith.com

Designed by Debra McQuiston
Printed and bound in Hong Kong

Gibbs Smith books are printed on either recycled, 100% post-consumer waste, FSC-certified papers or on paper produced from sustainable PEFC-certified forest/controlled wood source. Learn more at www.pefc.org.

Library of Congress Cataloging-in-Publication Data

Ryan, Bill.
  Dutch oven cajun and creole / Bill Ryan ; photographs by Zac Williams. — 1st ed.
     p. cm.
  Includes index.
  ISBN 978-1-4236-2525-4
  1. Cooking, Creole—Louisiana style. 2. Cooking, American—Louisiana style. 3. Cooking, Cajun 4. Dutch oven cooking. I. Title.
  TX715.2.L68R925 2012
  641.59763—dc23
                                        2012009985

CONTENTS

DUTCH OVEN COOKING

From the early days of discovering the Americas, the Dutch oven has been utilized for cooking in everyday life. No one really knows who invented the first Dutch oven, but a silversmith named Paul Revere is credited with making changes by adding the three legs on the bottom and a flanged lid. With new technology providing other materials such as stainless steel or Teflon, the use of cast iron for everyday cooking started to decline in the 1950s. But over the last several decades, groups of folks have formed societies with the purpose of preserving the art of Dutch oven cooking. Why cook in Dutch ovens? Because it's fun, easy to do, and the food tastes great.

THE RIGHT OVEN

When I teach a "Cast Iron 101" workshop, there are two questions always asked: "What size oven do I need?" and "How do I control the temperature?" Let's look at getting the right oven first. There are several manufactures of ovens on the market today. The two most popular are Lodge and Camp Chef, but there are also several other brands that are available. Whichever you choose, there are a few basic things to look for in a Dutch oven.

The walls and bottom of the oven should have a smooth finish inside and out, with no marks, deep scratches, cracks, or grind marks. The lid should fit snugly all the way around with no gaps. New ovens will either be seasoned or unseasoned. If the oven is unseasoned, when you inspected it, you will notice a light wax coating that has been applied to keep the oven from rusting.

Many sporting goods stores carry Dutch ovens and you can also find bargains at garage sales or flea markets. The chart on page 6 will give you an idea of about what size you need to purchase based on the number of servings you will need. The most common size is a 12-inch Dutch oven.

OVEN SIZE	OVEN CAPACITY	SERVING SIZES
8-inch	2 quarts	Main dish for 2–4 servings Side dish for 6–10 servings
10-inch	4 quarts	Main Dish 2–8 servings Side dish 10–12 servings
12-inch	6 quarts	Main dish 6–10 servings Side dish 12–16 servings
12-inch deep	8 quarts	Main dish 6–14 servings Side dish 16–22 serving
14-inch	8 quarts	Main dish 6–14 servings Side dish 16–22 servings
14-inch deep	10 quarts	Main dish 12–22 servings Side dish 18–26 servings
16-inch	12 quarts	Main dish 26–36 servings Side dish 48–60 servings

SEASONING THE OVEN

New ovens today are already seasoned; you can take them right out of the box and start using them. If you purchase an oven that is not, you will need to cure or season it before cooking with it. The first step is to wash it with soap and hot water to remove the thin coat of wax that has most likely been applied to it. Then dry your oven with a little heat, just enough to remove any excess water. Using lard, bacon grease, or cooking oil, cover the oven to include the lid, inside and out, with a light coat. Place the oven either in your house oven, grill, or some other covered heat source at 400 degrees for 1 hour. Allow the oven to cool, about 2 hours, apply a second coat of grease, and heat again at 400 degrees for another hour. If you are seasoning your Dutch oven in the house, beware that the smell will be similar to when you self-clean an oven.

Your oven is now ready for cooking. For the first couple of times using a newly seasoned Dutch oven, avoid cooking anything that is high in acid. This will help in building up the coating on the oven. Overtime, with continued use of your oven, the pores will fill, creating a smooth nonstick surface.

CLEANING YOUR DUTCH OVEN

If you take care of your ovens, they will last for generations. There are several methods for cleaning Dutch ovens. I recommend that once your oven is seasoned; never use any type of soap. I clean my pots by using heat and a vinegar-water solution (1 part vinegar to 4 parts water). Clean your ovens while they are warm, you might need to reheat them, by scraping out any remaining food using a plastic scraper. Spray with the vinegar solution and scrub with a nylon brush to remove any remaining food particles. Leave the oven on the heat to dry out any moisture and then set aside and cool. Coat the oven with a light layer of oil. I use mineral oil as it will not go rancid when stored. However, you can use vegetable oil if you choose.

Another method of cleaning your pot is to place it on a heat source and add a small amount of water. Once the water is heated, but not boiling, scrub with a nylon brush and repeat until the oven is clean. Then oil the oven for storage.

Some folks say that you don't need to oil your ovens; this will depend on where you live. Being in the south and high humidity, we have to put on a light coat of oil or the oven will rust.

STORING YOUR DUTCH OVEN

Once you have cleaned your oven; place a paper towel or coffee filter inside the oven. This will absorb any moisture that is left in the cast iron. Fold a paper towel or coffee filter several times, place over the edge, and put the lid on. This will allow the oven to breathe and prevent a moisture chamber from forming inside. You can store your oven in custom made bags, the original box, or even design a wooden box. This also aids in transportation of the ovens.

HOW TO CONTROL THE HEAT

The hardest part of using a Dutch oven is learning how to control the heat. There are many different methods that can be used. Try different ways of heating your pot until you find a style that fits your needs. Here is the method that I teach; it's called the "Rule of 3." Take the size of the oven that you are going to use, let's say a 12-inch oven, and use

3 less coals on the bottom than the number of inches and 3 more coals than the number of inches on the top. That would be 9 coals on the bottom and 15 coals on the top. This will yield an internal temperature of about 325 degrees. For every 2 coals you add, the heat will increase about 25 degrees.

While coals do not provide the exact temperature like your home oven does, they get close. Remember that weather conditions will affect how the coals burn. You have to take the weather into account when cooking. On cold or windy days, the coals are going to burn quickly, and on damp or rainy days, the coals will put out a little less heat. Practice will make you more comfortable cooking when the weather is not sunny.

Coal placement is another issue where it comes down to what you prefer. I use a single ring around the bottom and single ring on the top. Until you are very good at cooking with coals, be careful placing them in the center of the ring on the bottom. It is very easy to burn your food that way. I try my best not to remove the lid during cooking; you will lose 25–50 degrees of heat when you remove the lid.

OTHER ITEMS YOU MIGHT NEED

Here are some items that will be very helpful to you as you enjoy cooking in your Dutch oven. A charcoal chimney starter for your coals; tongs to move hot coals around; a table to cook on, you can either purchase one or make your own; heavy gloves to protect your hands; a lid lifter such as a claw hammer to remove the lid; and a lid stand to place your lid on when it's hot. Over time you will discover other items to add to your outdoor cooking experience.

Attend a Dutch Oven Gathering (DOG) in your area. A DOG is nothing more than folks getting together and cooking. Normally the ovens are placed on a table and served buffet style. It's a great way to meet new folks. You will also get to see other techniques for cooking in Dutch ovens; as well as different items to enhance the experience. I have listed several websites in the resources section were you can find equipment and groups to cook with.

IT'S ALL ABOUT THE FOOD

Growing up in the southern United States, I learned that many different cultures and traditions influenced the food we prepare and eat. These influences came from Scottish, Irish, French, Native American, British, African American, and Spanish cuisines. The American Indian tribes of the Caddo, Choctaw, and Seminole provided food items such as squash, tomatoes, corn, and a southern favorite, grits. They also influenced the use of slow cooking food and the utilization of potatoes, pumpkin, different types of beans, as well as fruits that flourish in the South. The African culture provided us with eggplant, nuts, okra, and black-eyed peas.

The early settlers of Louisiana infused these influences with their own traditions and created Creole and Cajun cuisines. Since the New Orleans area was a major harbor for immigrants and supplies to the south, Creole cooking was blended from French, Spanish, Portuguese, Italian, Greek, Asian Indian, American Indian, and African cultures. Part of this influence involves the use of bell peppers, rice, beans, and most importantly, tomatoes.

Creole dishes today use tomato as a base served over rice.

Cajun cuisine developed in the Acadian region of Louisiana. The early settlers in this area were deported by the British from the French-held region of Acadia in Canada. These settlers used whatever ingredients were available. It was soon discovered that rice could grow in this area year round and was quickly incorporated into the daily diet. It was in this area that crawfish, sugar cane, and sassafras, along with game meats made their way to the cooking pot. A typical Cajun meal consists of a main dish, rice, cornbread, and a vegetable.

A common trait in both Creole and Cajun styles of cooking is the use of the "holy trinity"—2 parts onion, 1 part green bell pepper, and 1 part celery that have been finely chopped. It is used in such dishes as etouffee, gumbo, and jambalaya.

When talking about Louisiana food, I have to write a little about gumbo and jambalaya. Having lived here since 1988, I was quickly taught that these are two completely different dishes and I had better not get them confused with each other.

Gumbo is a soup or stew that is made from a meat or seafood stock, a thickener called roux (pronounced roo), and the holy trinity. Okra is added to some gumbos to create a thicker variety. No Louisianan would dream of making gumbo without a roux. The browning of the flour takes away the raw pasty taste of white flour and gives it a nut-like roasted flavor that is so wonderfully Creole.

A roux is simply a mixture of flour and fat cooked and stirred until it is brown. Slowly heating the flour breaks up the starch molecules and reduces its thickening power while giving it a unique scorched flavor at the same time. The degree of doneness is determined by the color, which gets darker the longer it is cooked.

After the roux is prepared, the vegetables are added and cooked down, and then the meat is added along with tomatoes and the stock. Gumbo is normally cooked for at least 3 hours. The last items added are the seafood and spices and then it is served over rice when ready.

Jambalaya is a dish consisting of meats, vegetables, stock, and rice. There are two basic types; Creole, that contains tomatoes, and Cajun, that doesn't. The most common jambalaya is Creole. You start the dish by adding meat, chicken or sausage, or both, the trinity, and tomatoes. These are cooked down then the rice and stock are added in equal portions and brought to a boil for a few minutes before simmering until the stock is absorbed and the rice is done. Don't worry; I have included a basic recipe for both.

The recipes contained in this book can easily be cooked indoors, but they will taste better cooked in a cast iron pot outdoors. If you decide to cook any of these recipes inside, simply follow the directions to include cooking temperatures and time. If you prefer to use your Dutch oven inside and it has feet, just place it on a baking sheet.

CAJUN SEASONINGS

CAJUN SEASONING

1 tablespoon dried thyme
1 tablespoon dried sweet basil leaves
1 tablespoon dried parsley
1 tablespoon sweet paprika
1/2 tablespoon garlic powder
1/2 tablespoon onion powder
1 teaspoon salt
1 teaspoon pepper
1 teaspoon white pepper

Combine all the ingredients and mix thoroughly. This seasoning is used in many of the recipes in this cookbook. You can also add it to any dish you want for a little extra heat.

MAKES 1/2 CUP

SEASONED FLOUR

2 cups flour
1/2 tablespoon salt
1 tablespoon celery salt
1 tablespoon pepper
2 tablespoons dry mustard
4 tablespoons paprika
2 tablespoons garlic salt
1 teaspoon ground ginger
1/2 teaspoon thyme
1/2 teaspoon basil
1/2 teaspoon oregano

Combine all ingredients in a large ziplock bag and shake until mixed. Use this mixture when a recipe calls for dredging a meat or vegetable with flour.

MAKES 2 1/2 CUPS

WHITE BUTTER ROUX

½ cup butter
½ cup flour

Melt butter over medium heat and whisk in flour, stirring constantly until flour and butter are well blended and bubbly. Do not brown. Use this in gumbos and sauces as a thickener.

MAKES 1 CUP

ROUX

1 cup butter or lard
1 cup flour

Melt the butter over medium heat and whisk in flour; stir until well blended. Keep stirring until the color you want is achieved. The darker the roux, the nuttier the flavor will be. Use this in gumbos and sauces as a thickener.

MAKES 2 CUPS

WHITE SAUCE

1 quart milk
1 small onion, diced
3 whole cloves
Pinch of thyme
6 whole peppercorns
2 small bay leaves
½ cup White Butter Roux
Salt and pepper, to taste
Pinch of nutmeg

In a 10-inch Dutch oven, heat milk over medium-high heat. Add onion, cloves, thyme, peppercorns, and bay leaves and continue to scald milk with seasonings for 20 minutes. DO NOT BOIL. Strain through cheese cloth and discard onion and seasonings.

Bring to a low boil and add roux. Stir constantly with whisk until mixture achieves a thickened sauce. Remove from heat and season with salt, pepper, and nutmeg.

MAKES 1 QUART

BREAKFASTS

MOUNTAIN MAN
BREAKFAST

12-inch Dutch oven
10 coals on bottom
16 coals on top
350 degrees

1 pound sausage
1 medium onion, chopped
1 medium green bell pepper, chopped
2 tablespoons olive oil
2 pounds hash brown potatoes
8 eggs, beaten
2 cups grated cheddar cheese

In a large skillet over a bed of coals (about 8–10 coals) or using a small camp stove, cook sausage until no longer pink. Add onion and bell pepper, cook until tender.

Coat bottom and sides of Dutch oven with olive oil and add hash browns, sausage mixture, and eggs; top with cheese. Cover and bake, using 10 coals underneath the oven and 16 coals on top, for 45 minutes or until toothpick inserted in center comes out clean.

SERVES 8–10

PRESNIK

12-inch Dutch oven
10 coals on bottom
16 coals on top
350 degrees

6 eggs, beaten
2 tablespoons sugar
1 teaspoon salt
1 cup milk
1 pound Monterey Jack cheese, cubed
3 ounces cream cheese
8 ounces cottage cheese
2 tablespoons butter, softened
1 tablespoon baking powder
1/2 cup flour

This recipe needs to be started the night before you want to serve it. Mix eggs, sugar, salt, and milk together in a medium bowl and refrigerate overnight. In another bowl, combine the cheeses and butter; refrigerate overnight.

In the morning, mix the baking powder and flour together and combine with the egg and cheese mixtures in a large bowl. Place in Dutch oven, cover, and bake, using 10 coals underneath the oven and 16 coals on top, for 40 minutes.

SERVES 8–10

COFFEE CAKE

10-inch Dutch oven
9 coals on bottom
15 coals on top
375 degrees

^{1}/$_4$ cup butter
^{1}/$_2$ cup sugar
1 egg, beaten
1 ^{1}/$_2$ cups flour
2 teaspoons baking powder
^{1}/$_2$ teaspoon salt
^{1}/$_2$ cup milk
1 egg yolk, slightly beaten
2 tablespoons heavy cream

Topping

^{1}/$_2$ cup brown sugar
3 tablespoons flour
1 teaspoon cinnamon
3 tablespoons butter
^{1}/$_2$ cup chopped nuts

In a large bowl, cream butter and sugar together; add egg and beat well. Add dry ingredients and milk and blend well. Pour batter into greased Dutch oven. Blend egg yolk and cream together in a small bowl and pour over top.

Combine all the topping ingredients in a small bowl and sprinkle over top of batter. Cover and bake, using 9 coals underneath the oven and 15 coals on top, for 30 minutes or until a toothpick comes out clean.

SERVES 5–7

CREOLE GRITS

10-inch Dutch oven
7 coals on bottom
13 coals on top
325 degrees

4 to 6 slices bacon
2 tablespoons flour
1/2 small onion, chopped
1/2 small green bell pepper, chopped
3 fresh tomatoes, peeled and chopped
1 cup quick grits
3 cups chicken broth
1 cup finely chopped ham
1 tablespoon Cajun Seasoning
(page 12), optional

In a large skillet over a bed of coals (about 8–10 coals) or using a small camp stove, fry bacon and retain 2 tablespoons of the drippings. Crumble bacon.

Place Dutch oven over about 12 coals and make a roux with the drippings and flour, stirring constantly until a light brown color. Be careful as it will burn quickly. Add onion and bell pepper; cook for 5 minutes and then stir in tomatoes and cook another 5 minutes. Add grits, broth, ham, and seasoning and stir. Cover and bake, using 7 coals underneath the oven and 13 coals on top, for 30–40 minutes or until grits are cooked.

SERVES 5–7

SAUSAGE
BREAKFAST TORTE

10-inch Dutch oven
7 coals on bottom
13 coals on top
325 degrees

1 cup baking mix*
1/2 cup yellow cornmeal
2 cups grated cheddar cheese, divided
1/2 cup chicken broth
8 eggs
1/4 cup half-and-half
1 teaspoon Cajun Seasoning (page 12)
1 tablespoon butter
1 teaspoon chopped mint
1 cup cooked pork sausage
1/3 cup crumbled feta cheese

In a medium bowl, combine baking mix, cornmeal, 1 cup cheese, and chicken broth. Spray bottom of Dutch oven with nonstick cooking spray and press mixture into bottom of oven, forming a crust. Cover and bake, using 7 coals underneath the oven and 13 coals on top, for 20 minutes

While the crust is baking, mix eggs, half-and-half, seasoning, butter, and mint in a large bowl. In a large skillet over a bed of coals (about 8–10 coals) or using a small camp stove, cook eggs until just soft and remove from heat; add sausage and feta cheese. Spread evenly over the crust and top with remaining cheese. Cover and bake, using the same coals, for an additional 20 minutes.

SERVES 5–7

*I prefer using Jiffy baking mix.

GRILLADES

10-inch Dutch oven
5 coals on bottom
11 coals on top
250 degrees

6 thin steaks or veal cutlets
2 to 4 tablespoons Cajun Seasoning (page 12), divided
1 cup flour
4 tablespoons olive oil
1 1/2 cups chopped onion
1 cup chopped green bell pepper
1/2 cup chopped celery
6 cloves garlic, chopped
3 medium tomatoes, chopped
2 cups beef broth
1/2 cup red wine
3 green onions, chopped

Tenderize the meat by flattening out with a meat hammer. Sprinkle both sides with Cajun Seasoning, rubbing into the meat. Mix flour and 1 tablespoon of Cajun Seasoning in a shallow bowl. Dredge meat through flour, coating well, and set aside. Reserve flour mixture.

In a large skillet over a bed of coals (about 8–10 coals) or using a small camp stove, warm oil to a medium heat and fry each steak very quickly on both sides; remove to a plate. Add 4 tablespoons of the flour mixture to the oil and stir to make a brown roux. When the desired color is reached, add the onion, bell pepper, celery, and garlic. Cook for about 5 minutes and then transfer contents of the skillet to the Dutch oven.

Stir in tomatoes, broth, and wine. Add remaining Cajun Seasoning and steaks. Cover and bake, using 5 coals underneath the oven and 11 coals on top, for 1 hour. When ready, place on a serving plate, add some sauce from the Dutch oven, and top with green onions. Serve with Creole Grits (page 21) or Cheese Grits (page 28).

SERVES 6

BEIGNETS

10-inch Dutch oven
15 coals on bottom
300 degrees

1 cup half-and-half
1 cup sugar
2 eggs
2 envelopes active dry yeast
1 cup butter, melted
5 cups flour
Cooking oil
Powdered sugar

In a small saucepan over a bed of coals (about 8–10 coals) or a small camp stove, heat the half-and-half with sugar, stirring until the sugar dissolves. Don't heat over 110 degrees.

In a large bowl, combine the eggs and yeast together and add in the sugar mixture. Stir in the butter until well combined. Add the flour, $1/2$ cup at a time, and stir until well absorbed. Let dough rise until double, about 1 hour.

Roll the dough out to about 1 inch thick and cut, using a small biscuit cutter or cut into squares. Cover with bread cloth and let double in size, about 1 hour.

Place Dutch oven over coals and heat about 2 inches of oil to 300 degrees. Carefully drop beignets in oil and cook for about 5 minutes, turning over halfway through time to ensure even cooking. Remove, drain, and sprinkle with powdered sugar.

SERVES 6–8

BLUEBERRY SAUSAGE BREAKFAST

12-inch oven
10 coals on bottom
16 coals on top
375 degrees

1/2 cup butter, melted
3/4 cup sugar
2 cups flour
1/2 teaspoon baking soda
1 teaspoon baking powder
2 eggs
8 ounces sour cream
1 pound pork sausage, cooked and drained
1 cup blueberries
1/2 cup brown sugar
1/2 cup chopped pecans or walnuts

Blueberry Sauce
2 tablespoons cornstarch
1/2 cup water
1/2 cup sugar
2 cups blueberries

In a medium bowl, stir butter and sugar until combined; add flour, baking soda, and baking powder and mix. Add eggs, one at a time, beating after each addition. Add sour cream and fold in sausage and blueberries. Pour into Dutch oven.

Stir brown sugar and pecans together in small bowl and add to top of dish. Cover and bake, using 10 coals underneath the oven and 16 coals on top, for 35–40 minutes. Serve with Blueberry Sauce.

BLUEBERRY SAUCE

In a small saucepan over a bed of coals (about 8–10 coals) or using a small camp stove, combine cornstarch and water, mixing until smooth. Add the sugar and blueberries and cook, stirring over medium heat until thick and bubbly. Cool slightly before using.

SERVES 6–8

CHEESE GRITS

10-inch Dutch oven
7 coals on bottom
13 coals on top
325 degrees

4 cups chicken broth
1 cup grits
1 teaspoon salt
4 tablespoons butter
2 cups grated cheddar cheese

Heat broth in Dutch oven over 12 coals and when almost ready to boil, add the grits and salt. Cover and cook, stirring occasionally, using 7 coals underneath the oven and 13 coals on top, for 30–35 minutes until grits are cooked. When done, remove from heat and add butter and cheese.

SERVES 5–7

PANCAKE
CASSEROLE

12-inch Dutch oven
11 coals on bottom
17 coals on top
375 degrees

¼ cup butter
2 cups baking mix
2 cups milk, divided
10 eggs, divided
2 cups grated cheddar cheese, divided
1 pound cooked ham, cubed
2 packages (6.5 ounces each) precooked sausage, chopped
1 tablespoon Cajun Seasoning (page 12)

Over a bed of coals (about 8–10 coals) or using a small camp stove, melt butter in Dutch oven. In a medium bowl, combine baking mix, 1 cup milk, 2 eggs, and half of the cheese; pour over butter. Add ham and sausage on top of the mix.

Mix remaining milk, eggs, and seasoning in a medium bowl and pour over casserole. Top with remaining cheese. Cover and bake, using 11 coals underneath the oven and 17 coals on top, for 30–40 minutes or until center is cooked through. Cool for 10 minutes before serving.

SERVES 6–8

CAJUN BREAKFAST CASSEROLE

12-inch Dutch oven
9 coals on bottom
12 coals on top
325 degrees

1 pound andouille or hot sausage,
cut into pieces
1 pound crawfish tails or shrimp
4 tablespoons butter
1/2 cup chopped onion
1/4 cup chopped green bell pepper
1/4 cup chopped celery
4 cloves garlic, chopped
12 eggs
1 cup milk
1 cup baking mix
1 cup grated cheddar cheese
2 tablespoons Cajun Seasoning
(page 12)

Place andouille, crawfish, and butter in Dutch oven over 14 coals. Cook for 5 minutes and then add the onion, bell pepper, celery, and garlic. Cook for additional 5 minutes.

In a large bowl, combine the eggs, milk, baking mix, cheese, and seasoning; pour over the andouille mixture. Cover and bake, using 9 coals underneath the oven and 12 coals on top, for 40–45 minutes or until center is cooked.

SERVES 6–8

BLOODY MARY BREAKFAST CASSEROLE

10-inch Dutch oven
9 coals on bottom
15 coals on top
375 degrees

12 slices white or wheat bread, crust removed, divided
3 cups grated pepper-jack cheese, divided
9 eggs
2 cups milk
1 jar (16 ounces) salsa

Grease bottom of Dutch oven, arrange 4 slices of bread on bottom, and cover with 1/3 of the cheese. Add another 4 slices bread, cover with half of the remaining cheese, and top with remaining bread.

In a large bowl, mix eggs and milk and pour over bread. Let stand for 30 minutes then pour on salsa and sprinkle with remaining cheese. Cover and bake, using 9 coals underneath the oven and 15 coals on top, for 30–40 minutes.

SERVES 5–7

MAIN DISHES

CREOLE PORK CHOPS

14-inch Dutch oven
12 coals on bottom
18 coals on top
350 degrees

6 thick-cut pork chops
2 cups chopped boudin (removed from casing)
3 tablespoons olive oil, divided
2 medium onions, sliced
2 cloves garlic, minced
1/4 cup chopped green bell pepper
1/2 cup white wine
2 to 3 tomatoes, diced
3 tablespoons lemon juice
1 1/2 tablespoons Worcestershire sauce
1 teaspoon salt
1/2 teaspoon pepper
1 bay leaf
Tabasco sauce, to taste
3 cups hot cooked brown rice

Make a slit into each pork chop and stuff with boudin. Secure with a toothpick. In Dutch oven over a bed of coals (about 8–10 coals) or a small camp stove, brown pork chops on both sides in 1 1/2 tablespoons of hot oil. Remove chops and discard oil.

Add remaining oil to Dutch oven and saute onions and garlic for 3 minutes. Add bell pepper and saute for 1 minute then add wine and bring to a boil, stirring to deglaze oven. Add tomatoes, lemon juice, Worcestershire sauce, seasonings, pork chops, and enough water to cover chops. Cover and simmer, using 12 coals underneath the oven and 18 coals on top, for 1 hour or until chops are tender, turning occasionally. Remove chops and bay leaf. Cook sauce until thickened to desired consistency. Spoon over chops. Serve over rice. This dish goes well with Cajun Mushrooms (page 81).

SERVES 6

STUFFED PORK TENDERLOIN

14-inch Dutch oven
10 coals on bottom
15 coals on top
350 degrees

3 to 5 pounds pork tenderloin
2 pounds andouille sausage
1 pound boudin
1 red bell pepper, thinly sliced
1 tablespoon Cajun Seasoning (page 12), divided
1 tablespoon pepper, divided
1 cup spinach leaves
1 onion

Butterfly tenderloin. Uncase sausage and boudin and chop; place in tenderloin. Cover with bell pepper slices. Sprinkle 1/2 of seasonings over meats and bell pepper. Cover with spinach. Roll tenderloin into a wrap then tie with butcher string. Cover outside of tenderloin with remaining seasonings.

Slice onion into thin rings and cover bottom of Dutch oven using half of the onions. Place tenderloin on top of onions and cover with remaining onions. Cover and cook, using 10 coals underneath the oven and 15 coals on top, for 1 1/2 hours. Replace coals after about 45 minutes to maintain correct temperature.

SERVES 8–10

BAKED COD
CAJUN STYLE

14-inch oven
10 coals on bottom
16 coals on top
300 degrees

1 cup butter
1 can (8 ounces) tomato sauce
1 teaspoon sugar
1 tablespoon Worcestershire sauce
1 cup chopped onion
1 cup chopped celery
1/2 cup chopped green bell pepper
4 cloves garlic, minced
4 pounds cod filets
4 tablespoons Cajun Seasoning (page 12)
1/4 cup dry white wine

In a medium saucepan over a bed of coals (about 8–10 coals) or a small camp stove, combine butter, tomato sauce, sugar, Worcestershire sauce, vegetables, and garlic to make a sauce. Cook over low heat for 1 hour.

Season fish with Cajun Seasoning and place in Dutch oven. Pour wine over fish and add sauce. Cover and cook, using 10 coals underneath the oven and 16 coals on top, for 1 hour, occasionally basting with sauce. Serve over Dirty Rice (page 48).

SERVES 6–8

CRAWFISH PIE

12-inch Dutch oven
8 coals on bottom
12 coals on top
300 degrees

1 pound crawfish tails
¼ cup butter
¾ cup chopped onion
¾ cup chopped green bell pepper
½ cup chopped celery
Cajun Seasoning (page 12), to taste
1 can (10.75 ounces) cream of mushroom soup
1 unbaked pie shell and top crust

In Dutch oven using a bed of coals (about 8–10 coals) or a small camp stove, saute crawfish in butter for 5 minutes. Add onion, bell pepper, and celery and saute for another 5 minutes. Add seasoning and then add soup; mix well. Allow to cool and thicken for 20 minutes. Transfer mixture from Dutch oven to a large bowl and clean oven.

Place mixture in pie shell and cover with top crust. Cut 4 slits in top, place pie in cleaned Dutch oven, cover, and bake, using 8 coals underneath the oven and 12 coals on top, for 30 minutes or until crust is brown. Cool for 10 minutes before serving.

SERVES 6–8

SPICED CHICKEN

12-inch Dutch oven
10 coals on bottom
16 coals on top
325 degrees

2/3 cup honey
6 tablespoons water
4 tablespoons prepared mustard
4 tablespoons butter, melted
4 teaspoons Cajun Seasoning (page 12)
4 teaspoons curry powder
2 teaspoons lemon juice
2 cloves garlic, minced
6 boneless chicken breasts
Hot cooked rice

In a large bowl, combine honey, water, mustard, butter, and dry seasonings; blend well and add lemon juice. Add chicken, turning to coat. Place in Dutch oven, cover, and bake, using 10 coals underneath the oven and 16 coals on top, for 30 minutes or until juices run clear. Serve over hot rice, topped with pan drippings.

SERVES 6

COKE BRISKET

12-inch Dutch oven
10 coals on bottom
16 coals on top
350 degrees

1 package dry onion soup mix
1 bottle (12 ounces) chili sauce
1 can (12 ounces) regular Coke
1 (4 to 5 pound) beef brisket

In a large bowl, combine soup mix, chili sauce, and Coke. Place brisket in Dutch oven, fat side up, and pour soup mixture over top. Cover and bake for 40 minutes per pound. Swap out coals every 60 minutes until meat is done using 10 coals underneath the oven and 16 coals on top.

SERVES 10–12

BARBECUE PORK MEDALLIONS

12-inch Dutch oven
10 coals on bottom
16 coals on top
350 degrees

2 pounds pork tenderloin,
cut $1/2$-inch thick
3 tablespoons olive oil
1 can (14 ounces) crushed tomatoes
$1/2$ cup ketchup
$1/4$ cup dark brown sugar
2 tablespoons Worcestershire sauce
2 tablespoons prepared mustard
1 tablespoon Cajun Seasoning
(page 12)

Preheat Dutch oven with 10 coals underneath the oven; add oil and sear pork medallions about 2 minutes per side. Remove pork, add all other ingredients and scrape bottom of oven to incorporate into sauce. Add medallions back to oven, cover, and cook, using 10 coals underneath the oven and 16 coals on top, for 1 hour.

SERVES 6–8

LOBSTER CREOLE

10-inch Dutch oven
7 coals on bottom
13 coals on top
325 degrees

1 cup chopped onion
1 clove garlic, crushed
2 small or 1 large green bell pepper, chopped
1/3 cup butter
1 can (3 ounces) tomato paste
8 medium or 5 large tomatoes, peeled and diced
3/4 cup white wine
1 bay leaf
1 tablespoon chopped parsley
2 tablespoons Cajun Seasoning (page 12)
1 teaspoon thyme
5 cups cooked lobster
Hot cooked rice

In Dutch oven, brown onion, garlic, and bell pepper in butter over a bed of coals (about 8–10 coals) or a small camp stove. Add tomato paste and tomatoes. Cover and simmer, using 7 coals underneath the oven and 13 coals on top, for 30 minutes.

Add wine, bay leaf, parsley, Cajun Seasoning, and thyme and simmer for 1 hour, stirring occasionally. Replace coals if needed to maintain temperature.

Uncover and simmer until sauce thickens, about 30 minutes using 10 coals underneath the oven. Add lobster and simmer an additional 15 minutes. Serve over rice.

SERVES 6–8

CAJUN CACCIATORE

12-inch Dutch oven
11 coals on bottom
17 coals on top
375 degrees

3 baking potatoes
2 pounds andouille or hot sausage cut into pieces
1 pound mushrooms, sliced
1 onion, chopped
2 cloves garlic, chopped
2 tablespoons olive oil
Cajun Seasoning (page 12), to taste
1 can (28 ounces) Rotel tomatoes with peppers

Cut potatoes into $1/2$-inch pieces and toss with sausage, mushrooms, onion, garlic, and olive oil in Dutch oven. Season to taste. Cover and bake, using 11 coals underneath the oven and 17 coals on top, for 30 minutes, occasionally stirring. Add tomatoes and cook an additional 30 minutes, or until potatoes are done.

SERVES 6–8

DIRTY RICE

10-inch Dutch oven
14 coals on bottom
14 coals on top
350 degrees

12 ounces pork sausage with sage
1 tablespoon extra-virgin olive oil
1/4 cup finely diced onion
1/4 cup finely chopped celery
1/2 green bell pepper, finely chopped
1 teaspoon poultry seasoning
1 package (6 ounces) long grain and wild rice with seasoning packet
2 1/3 cups low-sodium chicken broth

In Dutch oven over a bed of coals (about 8–10 coals) or a small camp stove, brown sausage then remove from oven and drain the grease.

Add the olive oil to Dutch oven. When hot, add the onion, celery, and bell pepper. Cook until vegetables are soft, about 3–5 minutes. Return sausage to oven, add poultry seasoning, and stir to combine. Add rice and seasoning packet and cook for 5 minutes, stirring frequently. Add chicken broth and bring to a boil, using 14 coals underneath the oven and 14 coals on top. Reduce heat to low by removing coals so that you have 8 coals underneath the oven and none on top. Simmer, covered, for 25 minutes or until rice is done.

SERVES 6–8

SEAFOOD BILL

12-inch deep Dutch oven
16 coals on bottom
350 degrees

1¼ pounds unpeeled, medium-size
fresh shrimp
½ cup butter
1 onion, chopped
1 green bell pepper, chopped
4 green onions, chopped
2 celery stalks, chopped
1½ tablespoons minced fresh garlic
1 tablespoon flour
1 can (14.5 ounces) diced tomatoes
1 can (10 ounces) whole tomatoes with
green chiles
1 can (6 ounces) tomato paste
⅔ cup water
1 pound cooked crawfish tails
½ teaspoon dried basil
½ teaspoon dried thyme
½ teaspoon dried oregano
½ teaspoon salt
¼ to ½ teaspoon ground black pepper
¼ to ½ teaspoon ground red pepper
Hot cooked rice

Peel shrimp, devein, and set aside.

Melt butter in Dutch oven, using 16 coals underneath the oven, then add vegetables and garlic, and saute over medium heat for 5 minutes or until tender. Add flour and cook, constantly stirring for 1 minute or until smooth. Stir in diced tomatoes, whole tomatoes, tomato paste, and water until blended; reduce heat by removing 8 coals and cook, stirring occasionally, for 30 minutes. Add shrimp, crawfish, and seasonings; cook, stirring occasionally, for 5 minutes or until shrimp turns pink. Serve over rice.

SERVES 6–8

CRAWFISH ETOUFFEE

12-inch Dutch oven
9 coals on bottom
15 coals on top
325 degrees

4 tablespoons butter
1 1/2 pounds crawfish tails or shrimp
Cajun Seasoning (page 12), to taste
1 onion, chopped
1/2 green bell pepper, chopped
2 cloves garlic, minced
2 teaspoons cornstarch
1 cup water
Hot cooked rice
1 tablespoon chopped green onions

Using a bed of coals (about 8–10 coals) or a small camp stove, melt butter in Dutch oven. Season crawfish with Cajun Seasoning and saute for 3 minutes. Add onion, bell pepper, and garlic to oven. Saute for 10 minutes.

Dissolve cornstarch in water and add to mixture. Cover and simmer, using 9 coals underneath the oven and 15 coals on top, for 20 minutes; stir and adjust seasoning. Serve over rice and top with green onions.

SERVES 10–12

CRAN-ORANGE
PORK TENDERLOIN

12-inch Dutch oven
10 coals on bottom
16 coals on top
350 degrees

¹/₄ teaspoon garlic salt
¹/₄ teaspoon pepper
¹/₈ teaspoon ground mustard
¹/₈ teaspoon ground cinnamon
1 (1 pound) pork tenderloin

Sauce
¹/₂ cup dried cranberries
¹/₄ cup orange juice, divided
¹/₈ teaspoon ground ginger
¹/₈ teaspoon cloves
1 can (11 ounces) mandarin oranges
1 tablespoon cornstarch

In small bowl, combine first 4 ingredients; rub over pork. Place on a wire rack inside Dutch oven, cover, and bake, using 10 coals underneath the oven and 16 coals on top, for 45–55 minutes or until meat thermometer reads 160 degrees.

SAUCE

In small saucepan, combine cranberries, ¹/₈ cup orange juice, ginger, and cloves. Drain oranges and reserve juice; set oranges aside. Add reserved juice to mixture and bring to boil over a bed of coals (about 8–10 coals) or a small camp stove. Reduce heat; cover and simmer for 5 minutes. Combine cornstarch and remaining orange juice until smooth, stir into sauce. Bring to boil; cook and stir for 1 minute or until thick. Fold in oranges. Serve over sliced pork.

SERVES 6–8

CAJUN JAMBALAYA

12-inch Dutch oven
16 coals on bottom
350 degrees

1 pound chicken, cubed
1 pound andouille sausage, sliced
1 medium onion, chopped
Salt and pepper, to taste
4 cups chicken broth or water
2 cups uncooked rice
1 teaspoon red pepper flakes

In Dutch oven over 16 coals, brown chicken and sausage for 15 minutes or until chicken juice runs clear. Add onion, salt, and pepper and saute for 5 minutes. Add chicken broth, rice, and red pepper; stir until well mixed. Remove 6 coals from underneath the oven, cover, and cook for 30 minutes. Stir and check to see if rice is done—broth should be completely absorbed. If not, cover and check about every 5 minutes until rice is cooked.

SERVES 8–10

Note: This is a basic recipe to build upon. You can add any other seasoning, celery, bell pepper, or meat you desire. Most folks add shrimp or other seafood instead of chicken.

CREOLE JAMBALAYA VARIATION

Follow the above recipe and add 2 cans (16 ounces each) diced tomatoes, with liquid, when you add the chicken broth. Reduce the broth by 1 cup.

CAJUN PORK ROAST

12-inch Dutch oven
9 coals on bottom
15 coals on top
325 degrees

1 cup finely chopped andouille sausage
1 cup finely chopped boudin (removed from casing)
1 to 2 cups grated Swiss cheese
1 (2 to 4 pound) boneless pork roast
Cajun Seasoning (page 12)
3 tablespoons cooking oil, divided
1 bag (4 to 6 ounces) small carrots
10 to 14 small red potatoes
1 onion, chopped
2 teaspoons flour
1 cup white wine
1/4 to 1/2 cup chicken stock
2 teaspoons thyme
8 ounces small portobello mushrooms, sliced
Salt and pepper, to taste
1/4 to 1/2 cup sour cream
1 tablespoon parsley

In a medium bowl, mix sausages together and add enough cheese to make moldable. Mold into 4 evenly sized balls and roll into lengths just short of pork roast. Slice roast 4 evenly spaced times, about 3/4 of the way through. Add rolled ingredients into each cut area. Secure with kitchen string or toothpicks and sprinkle with seasoning. In Dutch oven, heat 1 tablespoon oil over 16 coals. Sear pork roast quickly so that it gets color, but the cheese doesn't melt. Remove and set aside.

Add carrots, potatoes, and onion to the oven and cook until onion is translucent and vegetables are softened. Add flour and stir to mix. Deglaze with wine and add roast along with stock and thyme. Cover and simmer, using 9 coals underneath the oven and 15 coals on top, for 1 1/2 hours, replacing coals after 45 minutes.

Remove roast from the oven once it's cooked. Remove carrots, onion, and potatoes, and reduce sauce for 5 minutes. Meanwhile, heat remaining oil in a small saucepan over a bed of coals (about 8–10 coals) or a small camp stove to high heat and add mushrooms. Toss to coat and season with salt and pepper. Cook mushrooms until golden, add to sauce, and then whisk in the sour cream. Serve sauce on side of roast with carrots and potatoes topped with parsley.

SERVES 8–10

ALLIGATOR PUFFS
WITH WHITE SAUCE

12-inch Dutch oven
9 coals on bottom
15 coals on top
350 degrees

1 pound chopped alligator
2 tablespoons cooking oil
1/2 cup diced onion
1/2 cup diced celery
1/2 cup diced red bell pepper
1 tablespoon minced garlic
1/2 cup sliced green onions
1/4 cup chopped parsley
1 tablespoon Pernod or Herbsaint
(ouzo)
2 tablespoons sherry
2 cups White Sauce (page 13), divided
1/2 to 1 cup Italian bread crumbs

Pouches
1/4 cup butter
2 tablespoons olive oil
1 box phyllo dough

In a large skillet using a bed of coals (about 8–10 coals) or a small camp stove, saute alligator in oil for 15 minutes; add onion and cook until translucent, about 10 minutes. Add bell pepper and garlic and simmer until gator is cooked, about 15 minutes more. Remove from heat and let cool. Add remaining ingredients, using 1 cup White Sauce.

POUCHES

In a small saucepan using a bed of coals (about 8–10 coals) or a small camp stove, melt the butter with oil over medium heat. Lay out 4 phyllo sheets, brushing each with the butter-oil mixture and cut each into 2 (5-inch) squares. Place about 1/4 cup of filling in center of each square. Lightly brush phyllo from edge of filling to each point of square with water. Gather points of square and pinch together just above filling. Brush pouch with butter-oil mixture.

Place filled pouches at least 1 inch apart in Dutch oven. Cover and bake, using 9 coals underneath the oven and 15 coals on top, for about 20–25 minutes or until golden brown. Serve warm pouches with remaining sauce.

SERVES 6

BAYOU CHICKEN WITH ANDOUILLE TARRAGON CREAM

12-inch Dutch oven
9 coals on bottom
15 coals on top
350 degrees

Chicken

6 boneless chicken breasts
Salt and pepper, to taste
1/2 pound chopped crawfish tails
1/4 cup each diced onions and celery
1/4 cup diced red bell pepper
1 tablespoon minced garlic
1/4 cup sliced green onions
1/4 cup chopped parsley
1/2 tablespoon Pernod or Herbsaint (ouzo)
1 tablespoon sherry
1/2 cup White Sauce (page 13)
1/2 cup Italian bread crumbs
1 cup Seasoned Flour (page 12)
1/2 cup cooking oil

Andouille Tarragon Cream

1/4 cup melted butter
1 tablespoon sliced shallots
1 tablespoon minced garlic
1/4 cup finely chopped andouille
1 tablespoon flour
1 tablespoon chopped tarragon
1 ounce white wine
1 1/2 cups heavy whipping cream
Salt and pepper, to taste

CHICKEN

Pound chicken breasts lightly to flatten then season with salt and pepper. In a large bowl, mix all other ingredients together except for flour and oil. Blend well and adjust seasoning as desired. Place a small amount of stuffing in center of each chicken breast, roll up, and secure with toothpicks. Dust lightly with flour and set aside.

Using a bed of coals (about 8–10 coals) or a small camp stove, heat oil in Dutch oven over medium heat, add chicken and brown all sides; drain off all but 1 table-spoon of oil. Cover and cook, using 9 coals underneath the oven and 15 coals on top, for 30–40 minutes.

ANDOUILLE TARRAGON CREAM

In a small skillet, heat butter over medium heat using a bed of coals (about 8–10 coals) or a small camp stove. Add shallots, garlic, and andouille. Saute 3–5 minutes and then blend in flour and tarragon. Deglaze with white wine. Stir in cream and reduce to half. Season with salt and pepper and pour over chicken.

SERVES 6

SHRIMP CREOLE

10-inch Dutch oven
7 coals on bottom
13 coals on top
325 degrees

¾ cup chopped onion
3 cups thinly sliced celery
1 cup chopped green bell pepper
¼ cup butter
1 can (16 ounces) chopped tomatoes
3 tablespoons brown sugar
2 bay leaves
1½ teaspoons salt
¼ teaspoon pepper
3 tablespoons lemon juice
2 pounds cooked shrimp

Saute onion, celery, and bell pepper in butter in Dutch oven over a bed of coals (about 8–10 coals) or a small camp stove for 15 minutes.

Add tomatoes, brown sugar, bay leaves, salt, and pepper; mix well. Cover and simmer, using 7 coals underneath the oven and 13 coals on top, for 30 minutes. Add lemon juice and shrimp. Simmer 6–10 minutes more or until shrimp are cooked through; discard bay leaves.

SERVES 6–8

SIDES

EVA'S LOADED
BAKED BEANS

(In memory of my sister Eva Marie 1960–1997)

12-inch Dutch oven
10 coals on bottom
16 coals on top
350 degrees

1 pound ground sausage, browned
1 large onion, chopped
1 large green bell pepper, chopped
1 cup brown sugar
¼ cup molasses
1 pound bacon, cut into pieces
1 tablespoon garlic salt
2 cans (24 ounces each) pork and beans

Combine all ingredients together inside Dutch oven. Cover and bake, using 10 coals underneath the oven and 16 coals on top, for 50 minutes. You can serve this hot or cold.

SERVES 18–24

SOUTHERN LOUISIANA RED BEANS

12-inch Dutch oven
20 coals on bottom
350 degrees

1 pound red kidney beans
Ham bone or hock
1 medium onion, chopped
1 small green bell pepper, chopped
2 bay leaves
2 cloves garlic, minced
$1/2$ tablespoon red pepper
1 teaspoon Tabasco sauce
1 pound smoked sausage, sliced into $1/4$ inch pieces
1 teaspoon salt
Hot cooked rice

Wash and sort beans, cover with water, and let sit over night.

Place beans in Dutch oven, including soaking water, and add ham, onion, bell pepper, bay leaves, garlic, red pepper, Tabasco sauce, sausage, and salt. Place Dutch oven over 20 coals, cover, and cook for 3–4 hours. Replace coals every hour until beans are tender and thick gravy has formed. Serve over rice.

SERVES 12–16

CORN AND GREEN
BEAN CASSEROLE

10-inch Dutch oven
9 coals on bottom
15 coals on top
375 degrees

1 can (16 ounces) shoepeg corn
1 can (16 ounces) French-style green beans
1/2 cup celery
1/2 cup green bell pepper
1/2 cup onion
1/2 cup sour cream
1 cup grated cheddar cheese
1 can (10.75 ounces) cream of celery soup

Topping
1/4 cup butter, melted
1 cup crushed Ritz crackers

In a large bowl, combine casserole ingredients and pour into Dutch oven. Combine topping ingredients in a small bowl and sprinkle over the top. Cover and bake, using 9 coals underneath the oven and 15 coals on top, for 1 hour.

SERVES 8–10

NEW ORLEANS RED BEANS

12-inch Dutch oven
20 coals on bottom
350 degrees

¾ pound kidney beans
½ pound salt pork, cut into cubes
1 tablespoon bacon drippings
1 tablespoon flour
1 large onion, chopped
1 carrot, thinly grated
3 pints chicken stock
Pinch of sage
Pinch of thyme
2 tablespoons parsley or 3 sprigs, chopped
3 stalks celery with leaves, chopped
Salt and pepper, to taste
Hot cooked rice

Wash and sort beans, place in a large saucepan, and cover with water. Let sit over night and then drain.

In Dutch oven using a bed of coals (about 8–10 coals) or a small camp stove, brown pork in bacon drippings and then remove. Add flour and cook, constantly stirring, until a light brown roux is achieved. Add onion and cook for about 3 minutes. Add beans, carrot, and pork. Pour in stock, cover, and cook for 1 hour over 20 coals, and then add herbs, celery, salt, and pepper. Cook until base is thick and serve over rice.

SERVES 12–16

BAKED CORN
CASSEROLE

10-inch Dutch oven
7 coals on bottom
10 coals on top
325 degrees

1 can (16 ounces) cream-style corn
1 can (16 ounces) whole kernel corn
1/2 cup yellow cornmeal
2 eggs, beaten
1 tablespoon garlic salt
1 teaspoon baking powder
1/4 cup cooking oil
2 cups grated cheddar cheese

In a large bowl, combine both kinds of corn together with cornmeal, eggs, garlic salt, baking powder, and oil. Mix in cheese and pour into Dutch oven. Cover and bake, using 7 coals underneath the oven and 10 coals on top, for 40–50 minutes.

SERVES 8–10

POTATOES
WITH APPLES

10-inch Dutch oven
7 coals on bottom
10 coals on top
325 degrees

1 medium onion, thinly sliced
6 medium potatoes, sliced 1/4-inch thick
3 Granny Smith apples, sliced 1/2-inch thick
Salt and pepper, to taste
8 ounces cheddar cheese, grated

Place layer of onion rings in bottom of Dutch oven. Cover with layer of potatoes then apples. Season and repeat layers twice. Cover and bake, using 7 coals underneath the oven and 10 coals on top, for 45 minutes; add cheese and cook 10–15 minutes more.

SERVES 8–10

SWEET AND SOUR
CABBAGE

12-inch Dutch oven
9 coals on bottom
15 coals on top
325 degrees

8 cups shredded cabbage
4 cups peeled and thinly sliced apples
½ cup brown sugar
½ cup apple cider vinegar
2 teaspoons salt
Ground pepper, to taste
1 tablespoon caraway seeds
½ cup water

Combine cabbage and apples in Dutch oven. In a small bowl, combine sugar and vinegar; stir until sugar dissolves. Add remaining ingredients. Pour over cabbage and apples. Cover and bake, using 9 coals underneath the oven and 15 coals on top, for 35–40 minutes. Stir before serving.

SERVES 10–12

CREOLE
GREEN BEANS

10-inch Dutch oven
8 coals on bottom
14 coals on top
350 degrees

1/2 **cup butter**
1 pound tasso
1 medium onion, finely chopped
2 pounds green beans
2 tablespoons chopped garlic
2 tablespoons Cajun Seasoning (page 12)

Over 8 coals, melt butter in Dutch oven. Add tasso, stir, and cook for 3–4 minutes. Add onion, beans, garlic, and seasoning. Cover and cook, using 8 coals underneath the oven and 14 coals on top, for 30 minutes or until beans are nice and tender

SERVES 8–10

HASH BROWN CASSEROLE

12-inch Dutch oven
10 coals on bottom
16 coals on top
350 degrees

1 pound sausage, cooked and drained
1 bag (30 ounces) shredded hash brown potatoes, thawed
1 small onion, chopped
2 cups sour cream
2 cans (10.75 ounces each) cream of potato soup
1 cup grated cheddar cheese

Combine sausage and hash browns in Dutch oven. Add onion and sour cream and mix in the soup and cheese. Cover and bake, using 10 coals underneath the oven and 16 coals on top, for 45 minutes.

SERVES 10–12

TATORS TWICE BAKED
WITH SHRIMP

12-inch Dutch oven
12 coals on bottom
18 coals on top
400 degrees

4 medium potatoes
1 can (10.75 ounces) cream of mushroom soup
1/4 cup milk
1 tablespoon Cajun Seasoning (page 12)
1 1/2 cups precooked shrimp or crawfish
1/2 cup grated cheddar cheese
Paprika, to taste

Bake potatoes at 400 degrees for 1 hour in Dutch oven using 12 coals underneath the oven and 18 coals on top.

Mix soup, milk, seasoning, shrimp, and cheese together in a medium saucepan and warm over a bed of coals (8–10 coals) or small camp stove, stirring until well blended.

After potatoes are cooked, cut in half and scoop out pulp. Mash potatoes in a large bowl and add the soup mixture. Stir until mixture becomes fluffy. Spoon into potato halves, sprinkle with paprika, and place in Dutch oven. Cover and bake, using 12 coals underneath the oven and 18 coals on top, for 15 minutes.

SERVES 8

SCALLOPED CORN
CASSEROLE

10-inch Dutch oven
7 coals on bottom
13 coals on top
325 degrees

2 eggs, beaten
2 tablespoons butter
1 cup milk
1 cup chopped onion
2 cloves garlic, minced
1/2 cup chopped red bell pepper
1 bag (10 ounces) frozen corn
1 can (16 ounces) cream-style corn
1 cup grated cheddar cheese

Topping
1 1/2 cups crushed saltine crackers
2 tablespoons melted butter

Mix eggs, butter, and milk together in Dutch oven. Add onion, garlic, bell pepper, and both kinds of corn to mixture. Mix in cheese, cover, and bake, using 7 coals underneath the oven and 13 coals on top, for 30 minutes.

Combine the topping ingredients together and add to top of casserole. Bake an additional 15 minutes.

SERVES 8–10

AUTUMN SWEET POTATOES

12-inch Dutch oven
10 coals on bottom
16 coals on top
350 degrees

3 to 4 pounds sweet potatoes, peeled and cut into 2-inch pieces
1 can (20 ounces) apple pie filling
1 cup golden raisins
1 tablespoon allspice
4 tablespoons butter, cut into pieces

Topping
1 cup chopped pecans
1/3 cup sugar
2 tablespoons butter

Layer sweet potatoes, apple pie filling, and raisins in Dutch oven. Sprinkle allspice over top and add butter. Cover and cook, using 10 coals underneath the oven and 16 coals on top, for 1 hour.

TOPPING

Combine pecans, sugar, and butter in a small saucepan and heat over medium heat using a bed of coals (10–12 coals) or small camp stove until sugar clings to nuts. Pour out on plastic cutting board to cool; chop and sprinkle on top of dish.

SERVES 12–14

HERB-ROASTED
NEW POTATOES

12-inch Dutch oven
9 coals on bottom
15 coals on top
350 degrees

1 pound new potatoes, quartered
¼ cup diced onion
¼ cup diced red bell pepper
¼ cup diced yellow bell pepper
1 tablespoon minced garlic
1 tablespoon chopped rosemary
1 tablespoon chopped thyme
¼ cup olive oil
¼ cup melted butter
2 tablespoons red wine vinegar
Salt and pepper, to taste
2 teaspoons Cajun Seasoning (page 12)

Place potatoes in a large ziplock bag. Add remaining ingredients and seal. Shake to mix and completely coat potatoes. Place in cooler until ready to cook.

When ready to cook, preheat Dutch oven to 350 degrees using 9 coals underneath the oven and 15 coals on top. Place potatoes in Dutch oven, cover, and cook, occasionally stirring, for 45–60 minutes or until potatoes are tender and golden brown.

SERVES 10–12

CAJUN MUSHROOMS

10-inch Dutch oven
7 coals on bottom
10 coals on top
325 degrees

2 cloves garlic, minced
1 teaspoon oregano
1 medium onion, diced
¼ cup red wine
1 medium green bell pepper, diced
1 jalapeno pepper, chopped
1 medium tomato, diced
½ pound whole button mushrooms
1 tablespoon tomato paste

In Dutch oven over 7 coals, simmer garlic, oregano, and onion in the wine for 5 minutes. Add bell pepper and jalapeno pepper. Cover and cook, using 7 coals underneath the oven and 10 coals on top, for 10 minutes, stirring frequently. Add tomatoes and simmer for 30 minutes. Add mushrooms and tomato paste and cook until the sauce is thickened, about 10–15 minutes.

SERVES 8–10

BREADS

CRAWFISH
FRENCH BREAD

14-inch Dutch oven
13 coals on bottom
19 coals on top
375 degrees

Crawfish Filling

1/4 cup butter
2 cups peeled crawfish tails
1/2 cup diced onion
1/2 cup diced celery
1/4 cup diced red bell pepper
1 tablespoon minced garlic
1/2 tablespoon dry mustard
1/2 cup mayonnaise
1/3 cup grated mozzarella cheese
1/3 cup grated cheddar cheese

Bread

3 cups bread flour, divided
1 1/4 envelopes active dry yeast
3/4 teaspoon salt
1 cup warm water (110 degrees)
1 egg white
1/2 teaspoon water
1/2 tablespoon cornmeal

CRAWFISH FILLING

In a large saucepan using a bed of coals (about 8–10 coals) or a small camp stove, melt butter; saute crawfish, onion, celery, bell pepper, and garlic for 15 minutes. Blend in mustard and mayonnaise. Add cheeses and blend together. Set aside.

BREAD

In a large bowl, combine 1 cup flour, yeast, and salt. Sir in water, blend well, and add remaining flour. Knead on floured surface for 8–10 minutes. Shape into ball, place in greased bowl, cover, and let rise for 1 hour. Punch down, cover, and let rise for 10 minutes.

Roll out dough into a 9 x 12-inch rectangle, spread with filling, and roll up. Beat egg white and water together and brush bread. Sprinkle inside of Dutch oven with cornmeal, place bread in oven, and let rise 35–40 minutes. Cut 3 diagonal slices in bread 1/4-inch deep. Cover and bake, using 13 coals underneath the oven and 19 coals on top, for 20 minutes. Brush with egg wash and bake an additional 20–30 minutes or until bread is done.

SERVES 10–12

SWEET DOUGH

14-inch Dutch oven
12 coals on bottom
18 coals on top
350 degrees

1 tablespoon yeast
1 cup warm water
$^1/_2$ cup warm milk
$^1/_2$ cup heavy cream
$^1/_2$ cup butter, melted
$^1/_4$ cup sugar
2 eggs, beaten
1 teaspoon vanilla
6 cups bread flour
$^1/_8$ teaspoon salt

In a large bowl, dissolve the yeast in the water and milk. Add the cream. Let stand for 5 minutes, or until the yeast is foamy.

Generously grease a large bowl.

Add the butter, sugar, eggs, and vanilla to the yeast mixture. Slowly add the flour and salt to the wet ingredients and mix well. Place dough on floured surface and knead for 4 minutes.

Place the dough in the prepared bowl, set in a warm dry place, and let dough rise for 1 hour. Punch down; use in a recipe or just make a loaf of bread.

To make bread, place dough in Dutch oven and let rise additional 1 hour. Cover and bake, using 12 coals underneath the oven and 18 coals on top, for 35–45 minutes or until golden brown.

SERVES 12–14

BAYOU BLAST BREAD

14-inch Dutch oven
12 coals on bottom
18 coals on top
350 degrees

1 cup butter
1/2 cup minced onion
1/2 cup minced green bell pepper
1 jalapeno, minced
1 jar (2 ounces) sliced pimentos
1 batch Sweet Dough (page 86)
Cajun Seasoning (page 12)
1/2 pound bacon, cooked and crumbled
1 cup Parmesan cheese

In a small saucepan using a bed of coals (about 8–10 coals) or a small camp stove, melt butter; stir in onion, bell pepper, and jalapeno. Saute until wilted then stir in pimentos.

Roll out dough into a 9 x 18-inch rectangle and divide into 3 equal sections. Sprinkle with seasoning. Spread onion mixture, bacon, and cheese evenly over all 3 sections. Roll up each piece of dough starting with the long side. Braid bread rolls together and coat with an egg wash mixture (1 egg and 2 tablespoons of water). Add more seasoning, if desired. Place in Dutch oven, cover, and bake, using 12 coals underneath the oven and 18 coals on top, for 35–45 minutes or until golden brown on top and cooked in the middle.

This bread is very tasty when served with Basil Butter. (Beat 1/2 cup softened butter with 4 tablespoons chopped fresh basil leaves.)

SERVES 12–14

SPICY SAUSAGE AND CHEESE ROLLS

12-inch Dutch oven
9 coals on bottom
15 coals on top
350 degrees

1/2 pound ground andouille or Italian sausage
1 cup minced yellow onion
1 tablespoon minced jalapeno
1 envelope dry yeast
2 tablespoons sugar
2 tablespoons plus 1 teaspoon cooking oil
2 cups warm water (about 110 degrees)
6 cups bread flour
3/4 cup yellow cornmeal, divided
2 teaspoons salt
1/2 pound white cheddar cheese, grated

In a medium skillet using a bed of coals (about 8–10 coals) or a small camp stove, brown sausage over medium heat. Add onion and jalapeno; cook for 3 minutes. Remove from heat and drain on paper towels. Set aside to cool.

Combine yeast, sugar, and 2 tablespoons oil in a small bowl. Add water. Mix to dissolve yeast. In a large mixing bowl, combine flour, 1/2 cup plus 2 tablespoons cornmeal, salt, sausage mixture, and cheese. Mix until it lightly comes together; add yeast mixture and stir until dough pulls from sides of the bowl and forms a ball. Remove dough and coat bowl with remaining oil. Return dough to the bowl and turn it to oil all sides. Cover with plastic wrap and let rise until double in size, about 2 hours.

Remove dough and turn on lightly floured surface. Using your hands, gently roll to form a narrow loaf about 24 inches long. Cut into 18 equal pieces. With the palm of your hand, roll the portions on a lightly floured surface to form small round rolls. Sprinkle bottom of Dutch oven with remaining cornmeal and place rolls in oven 1 inch apart. Let rise 30 minutes. Using a sharp knife, make an X on top of each roll. Cover and bake, using 9 coals underneath the oven and 15 coals on top, until golden brown, about 20 minutes.

MAKES 18 ROLLS

LOUISIANA STROMBOLI

12-inch Dutch oven
9 coals on bottom
15 coals on top
350 degrees

4^1/$_2$ cups bread flour
2^1/$_2$ teaspoons active dry yeast
2 teaspoons sea salt
3 tablespoons olive oil
1^1/$_2$ cups lukewarm water

Filling

6 ounces chopped cooked crawfish tails
1 cup diced jalapeno cheese
^{1}/$_2$ cup basil leaves
1 red bell pepper, diced
2 tablespoons Cajun Seasoning
(page 12)

In a large bowl, combine flour, yeast, salt, oil, and enough water to form a soft dough. Knead for 10 minutes, cover, and let rise for 1 hour. Knead for 2–3 minutes and let stand 10 minutes. Roll out dough into a 9 x 12-inch rectangle.

In a medium bowl, combine filling ingredients. Spread the filling evenly over dough and roll up. Cover for 10 minutes. Pierce the roll in several places. Brush with oil and sprinkle with a little salt. Place in Dutch oven, cover, and bake, using 9 coals underneath the oven and 15 coals on top, for 35–45 minutes, or until firm and golden in color. Serve fresh and warm, cutting into thick slices.

SERVES 10–12

RUBEN RYE BREAD

12-inch Dutch oven
10 coals on bottom
16 coals on top
350 degrees

Rye Bread

2 envelopes dry yeast

2 tablespoons sugar

3 tablespoons melted butter

1 egg

1 cup warm milk (about 110 degrees)

1 cup rye flour

$1^1/_2$ teaspoons salt

1 teaspoon cooking oil

$2^1/_2$ cups bread flour

1 tablespoon caraway seeds

1 large egg, beaten

Filling

$^1/_4$ cup Thousand Island dressing

$^1/_2$ pound corned beef, shredded

$^1/_2$ cup sauerkraut (drained and press as much liquid out as possible)

$^1/_2$ cup grated Swiss cheese

RYE BREAD

In a large bowl, combine yeast, sugar, butter, egg, and milk. Add the rye flour, salt, oil, bread flour, and caraway seeds. Beat mixture until ball forms. Use hands to form into a smooth ball. Lightly oil another large bowl, add dough, and turn to oil all sides. Place in warm, draft free area. Let rise about 1 hour or until double in size.

FILLING

Knead dough on lightly floured surface. Roll out into a 9 x 12-inch rectangle. Spread a light coating of Thousand Island dressing to within 1 inch of edge. Place corned beef on top then add sauerkraut. Top with cheese. Roll bread up and tuck ends. Place in Dutch oven seam side down, cover, and bake using 10 coals underneath the oven and 16 coals on top, for 50 minutes.

SERVES 10–12

TURKEY AND WILD RICE BREAD

14-inch Dutch oven
11 coals on bottom
17 coals on top
375 degrees

2 tablespoons butter
1 1/2 cups chopped cooked turkey
2 cups prepared long grain-wild rice blend
2 tablespoons lemon pepper, divided
Salt, to taste
2 cups grated cheddar cheese, divided
1 batch Sweet Dough (page 86)
2 tablespoons olive oil
2 tablespoons butter, melted
1 egg
1 tablespoon water

In a medium saucepan using a bed of coals (about 8–10 coals) or a small camp stove, melt butter over medium-low heat. Add the turkey, rice, 1 tablespoon lemon pepper, and salt. Mix well. Add 1 cup cheese and mix well.

Roll out dough into a 10 x 14-inch rectangle so that the long side is perpendicular to your body. With your hands, spread olive oil over the dough. Sprinkle the remaining lemon pepper and salt, to taste, evenly over the dough. Add the remaining cheese. Evenly distribute the turkey and rice mixture over the cheese and drizzle with butter.

With your hands, tightly roll the dough into a loaf with the rolling action going away from your body. Fold in outer edges as you roll. Place the loaf into Dutch oven seam side down. Beat together the egg and water to make an egg wash and brush over the dough. Cover and bake, using 11 coals underneath the oven and 17 coals on top, for 40–45 minutes.

SERVES 12–14

HONEY CHEDDAR
BISCUITS

12-inch Dutch oven
14 coals on bottom
20 coals on top
450 degrees

3 cups baking mix
1 cup milk
2 tablespoons honey
1/4 cup butter, melted
8 ounces sharp cheddar cheese, grated

Preheat Dutch oven using 14 coals underneath the oven and 20 coals on top.

In a medium bowl, combine baking mix, milk, honey, and butter; mix well and let stand for 5 minutes. Turn out dough onto a floured surface and knead several times. Roll dough out to 1/2-inch thickness and cut with round cutter. Place biscuits in Dutch oven, cover, and bake for 10–12 minutes using the same coals.

SERVES 10–12

SWEET POTATO CORNBREAD

10-inch Dutch oven
11 coals on bottom
17 coals on top
425 degrees

½ cup mashed sweet potato
¾ cup flour
1¼ cups cornmeal
3 teaspoons baking powder
1 teaspoon salt
½ cup sugar
½ teaspoon cinnamon
½ teaspoon nutmeg
1¼ cups buttermilk
2 eggs
2 tablespoons cooking oil, divided

Begin preheating Dutch oven when you start recipe by using 11 coals underneath the oven and 17 coals on top.

In a large bowl, mix all ingredients together except for 1 tablespoon oil. After about 20 minutes of heating oven, add remaining oil, spreading on bottom of oven. Heating the oven first and adding the oil will create a dark brown crusty/crunchy bottom. Add cornbread mixture, cover, and bake for 10–15 minutes or until firm in center using the same coals.

SERVES 8–10

CRAWFISH CORNBREAD

10-inch Dutch oven
11 coals on bottom
17 coals on top
425 degrees

1 pound crawfish tails
³/₄ cup chopped onion
¹/₄ cup butter
1 box (6 ounces) Martha White Cornbread Mix
¹/₂ teaspoon baking soda
¹/₂ teaspoon baking powder
1 teaspoon salt
2 eggs
1 cup milk
¹/₂ pound jalapeno cheese, grated

In a medium saucepan, saute crawfish and onion in butter using a bed of coals (about 8–10 coals) or a small camp stove

In a large bowl, combine cornbread mix, baking soda, baking powder, salt, and eggs then add milk, crawfish mix, and cheese. Pour into greased Dutch oven, cover, and bake, using 11 coals underneath the oven and 17 coals on top, for 45 minutes.

SERVES 8–10

SUPER QUICK ROLLS

12-inch Dutch oven
14 coals on bottom
20 coals on top
450 degrees

1 cup of milk
$^1/_2$ cup of water
$^1/_4$ cup plus 2 tablespoons butter

4 tablespoons sugar
2 envelopes active dry yeast
$3^1/_2$ to 4 cups bread flour

Combine milk, water, and $^1/_4$ cup butter in a small saucepan and warm using a bed of coals (about 8–10 coals) or a small camp stove until butter melts. Cool to 100–110 degrees and dissolve sugar and yeast into mixture.

Transfer to a large bowl and add $^1/_2$ cup flour at a time, stirring until moist. Knead for 5 minutes. Place in a well-oiled bowl, turning to coat ball of dough. Let rise 20 minutes. Punch down and shape into 20–24 balls. Place in Dutch oven and let rise another 20 minutes. Cover and bake, using 14 coals underneath the oven and 20 coals on top, for 14–18 minutes. After 8 minutes; brush the tops with remaining butter.

MAKES 20–24 ROLLS

MARDI GRAS ROLLS

12-inch Dutch oven
10 coals on bottom
16 coals on top
375 degrees

Filing

8 ounces cream cheese, softened
$1/2$ cup melted butter
2 to 4 teaspoons ground cinnamon

Bread

1 container (16 ounces) sour cream
$1/3$ cup plus 1 tablespoon sugar, divided
$1/4$ cup butter
1 teaspoon salt
2 envelopes active dry yeast
$1/2$ cup warm water (100–110 degrees)
2 eggs, slightly beaten
6 to $6^1/2$ cups bread flour, divided

Cream Glaze

3 cups powdered sugar
3 tablespoons butter, melted
2 tablespoons fresh lemon juice
$1/4$ teaspoon vanilla extract
2–4 tablespoons milk
Purple, yellow, and green colored sugars

FILING

Combine all ingredients, mix well, and set aside.

BREAD

Using a bed of coals (about 8–10 coals) or a small camp stove, cook sour cream, $1/3$ cup sugar, butter, and salt in a medium saucepan over low heat, stirring often, until butter melts. Set aside and cool mixture to 100–110 degrees. Stir together yeast, water, and remaining sugar in measuring cup, let stand 5 minutes or until yeast foams.

Beat sour cream and yeast mixtures, eggs, and 2 cups flour until smooth. Add remaining flour, $1/2$ cup at a time, until soft dough forms. Place dough onto lightly floured surface; knead until smooth and elastic, 10 minutes. Place in a greased bowl, turning to coat, cover, and let rise in warm place for about 1 hour or until double in size.

Punch down and divide in half. Roll out into a 12 x 22-inch rectangle, spread half of filling over dough, and roll up. Cut into 2-inch rolls. Repeat with other half of dough. Let rolls rise 20–30 minutes or until doubled. Place in Dutch oven, cover, and bake, using 10 coals underneath the oven and 16 coals on top, for 20–30 minutes. Remove from oven and let cool for 10 minutes.

CREAM GLAZE

Combine all ingredients except sugars and stir until smooth. Drizzle over top of rolls and sprinkle with sugars.

SERVES 10–12

JALAPENO CORNBREAD

10-inch Dutch oven
11 coals on bottom
17 coals on top
425 degrees

1 cup yellow cornmeal
$1/2$ teaspoon garlic powder
1 teaspoon baking powder
1 tablespoon Cajun Seasoning (page 12)
1 can (6 ounces) cream-style corn
1 cup plain yogurt
2 eggs, beaten
$2/3$ cup cooking oil
1 cup grated cheddar cheese
3 to 4 medium jalapeno peppers, finely chopped

In a large bowl, combine cornmeal, garlic powder, baking powder, and seasoning. Add corn and yogurt. Add eggs, oil, cheese, and peppers. Pour into Dutch oven, cover, and bake, using 11 coals underneath the oven and 17 coals on top, for 20–25 minutes.

SERVES 8–10

HAWAIIAN
SWEET BREAD

10-inch Dutch oven
9 coals on bottom
15 coals on top
375 degrees

7½ cups bread flour, divided
¾ cup potatoes flakes
⅔ cup sugar
2 envelopes active dry yeast
1 teaspoon salt
½ teaspoon ground ginger
1 cup milk
½ cup water
½ cup butter, softened
1 cup pineapple juice
3 eggs
2 teaspoons vanilla

In a large mixing bowl, combine 3 cups flour, potato flakes, sugar, yeast, salt, and ginger.

Using a bed of coals (about 8–10 coals) or a small camp stove, heat the milk, water, butter, and pineapple juice to 120–130 degrees in a small saucepan. Add to dry ingredients; beat just until moistened. Beat in eggs until smooth. Beat in vanilla and stir in enough flour to form soft dough.

Turn onto floured surface; knead until smooth and elastic, about 6–8 minutes. Place in a greased bowl, turning once to grease top. Cover and let rise in a warm place until double in size, about 1¼ hours. Punch dough down. Turn onto lightly floured surface and divide into thirds. Shape each third into a ball. Place in 3 greased 9-inch round baking pans. Cover; let rise until double, about 45 minutes. Bake, using 9 coals underneath the oven and 15 coals on top, for 20–25 minutes or until golden brown. Cover loosely with foil if tops brown too quickly.

MAKES 3 LOAVES

DESSERTS

PEPPERMINT CHOCOLATE CAKE

10-inch Dutch oven
7 coals on the bottom
13 coals on the top
325 degrees

Cake

3/4 cup unsalted butter
6 ounces semisweet chocolate, chopped
1 1/2 cups sugar
3 eggs
1 1/2 teaspoons peppermint extract
1 teaspoon vanilla
2 1/4 cups cake flour
1 teaspoon baking soda
3/4 teaspoon baking powder
3/4 teaspoon salt
1 1/2 cups sour cream

Frosting

1/2 cup unsalted butter
1 package (8 ounces) cream cheese, softened
3 1/2 cups powdered sugar, or more as needed

Glaze

1 ounce semisweet chocolate, chopped
1 tablespoon butter
1/2 teaspoon vanilla

CAKE

Line bottom of Dutch oven with parchment paper then grease and flour paper. Using a bed of coals (about 8-10 coals) or small camp stove, melt butter and chocolate in a small saucepan until smooth. Pour into large bowl; cool 10-15 minutes.

Beat sugar into chocolate then beat in eggs, peppermint extract, and vanilla. Whisk flour, baking soda, baking powder, and salt in medium bowl. Alternately beat sour cream and flour mixture into chocolate mixture, starting with sour cream. Pour into Dutch oven, cover and bake, using 7 coals underneath the oven and 13 coals on top, until toothpick comes out clean from center. Let cake cool in Dutch oven for 10-15 minutes then remove from oven. Cool completely on wire rack.

FROSTING

Beat butter and cream cheese in a medium bowl until smooth and creamy. Slowly mix in powdered sugar until well blended. Frost cooled cake.

GLAZE

In a small saucepan using a bed of coals (about 8-10 coals) or small camp stove, melt chocolate and butter, and stir until smooth. Cool until slightly thickened. With small fork or whisk, drizzle glaze over cake.

SERVES 12

RING-OF-COCONUT FUDGE CAKE

10-inch Dutch oven
8 coals on bottom
14 coals on top
350 degrees

Filling

1/4 cup sugar
1 teaspoon vanilla
8 ounces cream cheese
1 egg
1/2 cup shredded coconut
1 cup chocolate chips

Cake

2 cups sugar
1 cup cooking oil
2 eggs
3 cups flour
3/4 cup cocoa
2 teaspoons baking soda
2 teaspoons baking powder
1 1/2 teaspoons salt
1 cup hot coffee
1 teaspoon vanilla
1 cup sour milk (add 1 tablespoon lemon juice to milk, let sit 10–15 minutes)
1/2 cup chopped nuts

Glaze

1 cup confectioners' sugar
3 tablespoons cocoa
2 tablespoons butter
2 teaspoons vanilla
1 to 3 tablespoons hot water

FILLING

In a medium bowl, beat sugar, vanilla, cream cheese, and egg until smooth. Stir in coconut and chocolate chips; set aside in refrigerator or cooler to firm up.

CAKE

In a large bowl, combine sugar, oil, and eggs. Beat 1 minute. Add remaining ingredients, except nuts. Beat 3 minutes. Stir in nuts. Pour half of batter into Dutch oven. Carefully spoon filling over batter in center. Top with remaining batter. Cover and bake, using 8 coals underneath the oven and 14 coals on top, for 70–75 minutes. Cool for 15 minutes then remove cake from Dutch oven. Cool completely.

GLAZE

Combine ingredients in a small bowl and mix until smooth. Drizzle glaze over cooled cake.

SERVES 12

DUMP
COBBLERS

12-inch Dutch oven
10 coals on bottom
16 coals on top
350 degrees

2 cans (12 ounces each) peach pie filling
1 yellow cake mix
1 can (12 ounces) root beer
(never use diet soda)

Place peaches in bottom of Dutch oven, cover with dry cake mix. Pour soda over cake mix, coating entire mix. Let stand for 30. Cover and bake, using 10 coals underneath the oven and 16 coals on top, for 1 hour.

SERVES 14–16

OTHER COBBLER OPTIONS

Apple pie filling, caramel cake, Vanilla Coke, and caramel squares on top

Apple pie filling, diced pears, spice cake, and root beer

4 mashed bananas, chocolate cake, and root beer

4 mashed bananas, spice cake, and root beer

Blueberry pie filling, lemon pudding cake, and root beer

Blueberry pie filling, pineapple cake, and Dr. Pepper

Cherry and blueberry pie fillings, yellow cake, and root beer

Cherry pie filling, chocolate cake, and root beer

Peach pie filling, orange cake mix, and orange soda

Raspberry pie filling, chocolate cake, and root beer

Pineapple pie filling, coconut cake, and root beer

Strawberry pie filling, yellow cake, and root beer

PIONEER
JOURNEY CAKE

12-inch Dutch oven
11 coals on bottom
17 coals on top
375 degrees

1 1/2 cups sugar
3/4 cup butter
2 1/4 cups apple cider
1 tablespoon baking soda
1 teaspoon cinnamon
1 teaspoon ground cloves
1/2 cup dried apples, finely chopped
4 1/2 cups flour

Prepare Dutch oven by greasing sides and bottom. In a large bowl, cream sugar and butter until light and fluffy. Mix in apple cider. Add baking soda, cinnamon, cloves, and dried apples. Blend in flour, 1/2 cup at a time. Beat until batter is well mixed, then pour into prepared Dutch oven, cover, and bake, using 11 coals underneath the oven and 17 coals on top, for 35–45 minutes.

SERVES 14–16

BREAD PUDDING
DOUGHNUT STYLE

12-inch Dutch oven
10 coals on bottom
16 coals on top
350 degrees

1 tablespoon butter
12 glazed doughnuts, cut into 1/2-inch pieces
3 cups milk
1/2 cup chopped dried apricots
1/2 cup chopped dried cranberries and/or sultanas
1/2 cup amaretto, whiskey, or warm water
3 eggs, lightly beaten
1/2 cup sugar
1 teaspoon vanilla
1/2 teaspoon salt
1 teaspoon ground cinnamon
1/2 teaspoon ground nutmeg

Sauce
2 tablespoons butter
2 tablespoons flour
1 cup water or 1/2 cup water and 1/2 cup amaretto
3/4 cup sugar
1 teaspoon vanilla

Grease Dutch oven with butter. Spread doughnut pieces evenly in pan.

Using a bed of coals (about 8–10 coals) or a small camp stove, heat milk in medium saucepan; add apricots, cranberries, and amaretto and simmer 5 minutes. Add eggs, sugar, vanilla, salt, cinnamon, and nutmeg to milk mixture. Be careful not to overheat or the eggs will cook. Pour mixture over doughnuts and evenly spread apricots and cranberries on top. Let stand for about 20 minutes to allow the liquid to absorb. Cover and bake, using 10 coals underneath the oven and 16 coals on top, for 1 hour. Let rest for 15 minutes before serving. Serve warm or cooled, with or without sauce.

SAUCE

In a small saucepan using a bed of coals (about 8–10 coals) or a small camp stove, melt butter and stir in flour until smooth. Gradually add water, sugar, and vanilla. Bring to boil; cook and stir for 2 minutes or until thickened.

SERVES 14–16

UPSIDE-DOWN APPLE PIE

10-inch Dutch oven
9 coals on bottom
15 coals on top
375 degrees

Piecrust
2 cups flour
1/2 teaspoon salt
6 tablespoons shortening
2 tablespoons cold butter
5 to 7 tablespoons orange juice

Filling
6 tablespoons butter, melted, divided
1/2 cup firmly packed brown sugar
1/2 cup chopped pecans
1 cup sugar
1/3 cup flour
3/4 teaspoon ground cinnamon
1/4 teaspoon ground nutmeg
8 cups thinly sliced Golden Delicious apples

Glaze
1/2 cup confectioners' sugar
2 to 3 teaspoons orange juice

PIECRUST

In a medium bowl, combine flour and salt. Cut in shortening and butter until crumbly. Gradually add orange juice, tossing with a fork, until dough forms a ball. Divide into 2 balls. Cover in plastic wrap and refrigerate at least 30 minutes. Roll out 1 ball of dough into a 12-inch circle and place in Dutch oven or in a pie pan that you place into the oven.

FILLING

In a small bowl, combine 4 tablespoons butter, brown sugar, and pecans; spoon into piecrust.

In a large bowl, combine sugar, flour, cinnamon, nutmeg, apples, and remaining butter and toss gently. Spoon on top of pecan mixture. Roll out second ball of dough and place on top of pie. Pinch edges together to seal and cut steam vents.

Cover and bake, using 9 coals underneath the oven and 15 coals on top, for 20 minutes. Cover edges loosely with foil. Bake 30 minutes longer or until apples are tender and crust is golden brown. Cool 15 minutes. Invert onto plate, combine glaze ingredients, and drizzle over pie, of desired.

SERVES 12

CARAMEL CINNAMON
APPLE PIE

10-inch Dutch oven
11 coals on bottom
15 coals on top
375 degrees

Piecrust
2 cups flour
1/2 teaspoon salt
6 tablespoons shortening
2 tablespoons cold butter
4 tablespoons orange juice
3 tablespoons vodka

Toppings
2/3 cup crushed cinnamon graham crackers
1/4 cup firmly packed brown sugar
3 tablespoons flour
1/3 cup butter, melted
1 cup whipping cream
1/3 cup sugar
1/2 cup Caramel Butterscotch Ice Cream Topping
1/3 cup finely chopped pecans

Apple Filling
6 to 8 apples, peeled and sliced
1 1/2 teaspoons lemon juice
1 cup sugar
6 tablespoons flour
1/2 teaspoon ground cinnamon
1/2 teaspoon ground nutmeg

Egg Wash
1 egg beaten with 1 tablespoon water

PIECRUST

In a medium bowl, combine flour and salt. Cut in shortening and butter until crumbly. Gradually add orange juice and vodka, tossing with a fork until dough forms a ball. Divide into 2 balls. Cover in plastic wrap and place in refrigerator or cooler for at least 30 minutes. Roll out 1 ball of dough into a 12-inch circle and place in Dutch oven or in a pie pan that you place into the oven.

TOPPINGS

In a small bowl, mix graham crackers, brown sugar, flour, and butter until crumbly. Set aside. Pour whipping cream into a medium bowl and beat, add sugar a little at a time. When whipped, add caramel and fold in pecans. Refrigerate before serving.

APPLE FILLING

In a large bowl, combine apples, lemon juice, sugar, flour, cinnamon, and nutmeg. Spoon filling into piecrust and sprinkle cracker topping over apples.

Roll out second ball of dough, place on top of pie, and pinch edges. Using a pastry brush, brush top of pie with egg wash. Cover and bake, using 11 coals underneath the oven and 15 coals on top, for 55 minutes or until apples are bubbling and crust is browned. While still hot, drizzle pie with additional caramel, if desired.

SERVES 12

CAJUN CAKE

2 (10-inch) Dutch ovens
9 coals on bottom of each oven
15 coals on top of each oven
350 degrees

2 cups cake flour
1 1/2 cups sugar
2 teaspoons baking soda
1 can (20 ounces) crushed pineapple, drained
2 eggs, well beaten

Frosting
1/2 cup butter
3/4 cup sugar
1/2 cup evaporated milk
1 cup shredded coconut
1 cup finely chopped pecans
1 teaspoon vanilla

Sift flour, sugar, and baking soda together in a large bowl. Add pineapple and eggs. Mix well. Equally divide the batter between both Dutch ovens. Cover and bake, using 9 coals underneath the ovens and 15 coals on the tops, for 30 minutes or until done.

FROSTING

In a medium saucepan using a bed of coals (about 8–10 coals) or a small camp stove, melt butter then stir in sugar and milk and bring to a boil. Cook for 1 minute and then add remaining ingredients. Punch holes in 1 cake using a wooden skewer or fork and spread with frosting. Place second cake on top of frosted cake and add frosting, allowing it to run down the sides.

SERVES 12

PEACHY-SPICE
UPSIDE-DOWN CAKE

12-inch Dutch oven
10 coals on bottom
16 coals on top
350 degrees

2 cups flour
1 cup sugar
1 teaspoon salt
1 teaspoon baking powder
$3/4$ teaspoon baking soda
$3/4$ teaspoon ground cloves
$3/4$ teaspoon cinnamon
$2/3$ cup shortening, melted
$1 1/2$ cups firmly packed brown sugar, divided
1 cup buttermilk
3 eggs
4 tablespoons butter
Sliced peaches, fresh or canned (enough to cover bottom of oven)
12 to 14 Maraschino cherries

In a large bowl, combine flour, sugar, salt, baking powder, baking soda, cloves, and cinnamon. Add shortening, $3/4$ cup brown sugar, buttermilk, and eggs and mix together.

Melt butter and remaining brown sugar in bottom of Dutch oven over 10 coals. Arrange peach slices in bottom and garnish with cherries placed round side down. Pour cake mixture over the peaches. Cover and bake, using 10 coals underneath the oven and 16 coals on top, for 15 minutes. Remove from bottom heat, cooking with top heat only, for 30–35 minutes or until golden brown. Test with toothpick. Let stand 2–3 minutes and then invert Dutch oven to remove.

SERVES 14–16

HONEY BUN CAKE

12-inch oven
9 coals on bottom
15 coals on top
325 degrees

1 box yellow cake mix
1/2 cup applesauce
1/4 cup cooking oil
2 eggs
1/3 cup egg whites
8 ounces sour cream
3/4 cup firmly packed brown sugar
1 tablespoon ground cinnamon

Icing
1 1/2 cup confectioners' sugar
2 tablespoons milk
1 tablespoon vanilla

Preheat Dutch oven using 9 coals underneath the oven and 15 coals on top for 10 minutes.

In a large bowl, combine the cake mix, applesauce, oil, eggs, egg whites, and sour cream. Stir with a spoon, approximately 50 strokes, or until most large lumps are gone. Pour half the batter into Dutch oven. Combine brown sugar and cinnamon and sprinkle over the batter in the oven. Spoon the other half of the batter into oven, covering the brown sugar and cinnamon. Swirl the cake with a butter knife until it looks like a honey bun. Cover and bake for 40 minutes or until done using the same coals.

ICING
In a small bowl, whisk together sugar, milk, and vanilla until smooth. Ice cake while warm.

SERVES 14–16

RICH CHOCOLATE
PECAN PIE

10-inch Dutch oven
8 coals on bottom
14 coals on top
350 degrees

Sweet Piecrust
1 1/2 cups plus 2 tablespoons flour
1 tablespoon sugar
1/2 teaspoon salt
1/2 cup cold butter, cut into 1/4-inch pieces
2 tablespoons shortening
3 tablespoons cold water, divided

Pie Filling
1 1/2 cups pecan pieces
1 cup semisweet chocolate chips
4 eggs, beaten
1/2 cup sugar
1/2 cup light brown sugar
1/2 cup corn syrup
1/2 teaspoon vanilla

Caramel Sauce
3/4 cup sugar
2 tablespoons water
1/2 teaspoon fresh lemon juice
1/2 cup heavy cream
2 tablespoons to 1/4 cup milk

SWEET PIECRUST

Sift flour, sugar, and salt into a large bowl. Using your fingers, work in butter and shortening until mixture resembles coarse crumbs. Add 2 tablespoons water and work in until incorporated and dough comes together. Add more water as needed to make a smooth dough, but don't over work. Form dough into a disk, cover in plastic wrap, and refrigerate for at least 30 minutes. Roll out dough into a 12-inch circle and place in Dutch oven or in a pie pan that you place into the oven.

PIE FILLING

Spread pecans and chocolate chips evenly on bottom of piecrust. In a medium bowl, whisk remaining ingredients together and pour over pecans. Cover and bake, using 8 coals underneath the oven and 14 coals on top, until the filling sets, 50–60 minutes. Cool before slicing.

CARAMEL SAUCE

Using a bed of coals (about 8–10 coals) or a small camp stove, combine sugar, water, and lemon juice in a medium saucepan and cook until sugar dissolves. Boil without stirring until mixture becomes a deep amber color. Don't let it burn. Carefully add the cream. Whisk to combine and remove from heat. Stir in 2 tablespoons milk then 2 more until pourable. Drizzle over slices of pie.

SERVES 12

LIME-COCONUT
BUTTERMILK PIE

10-inch Dutch oven
10 coals on bottom
14 coals on top
350 degrees

1 piecrust
1 1/2 cups sugar
3/4 cup shredded coconut
1/2 cup buttermilk
1/2 cup unsweetened coconut milk
1 tablespoon flour
2 eggs
2 egg yolks
1/2 teaspoon vanilla
1 lime, zested and juiced
Pinch of salt

Line bottom of Dutch oven with piecrust.

In a large bowl, mix all ingredients together in order. Fill the piecrust, cover, and bake, using 10 coals underneath the oven and 14 coals on top, for 40–50 minutes or until the filling is set. Remove from heat, let cool 30 minutes, and then remove from Dutch oven.

SERVES 12

Hint: Place about 6 strips of parchment paper crisscrossed across the bottom of the Dutch oven and sticking up above the pie to allow you to remove it from the oven.

RUM CAKE

10-inch Dutch oven
7 coals on bottom
13 coals on top
325 degrees

1 yellow cake mix
1 small package instant French vanilla pudding mix
1/2 cup water
1/2 cup cooking oil
1/4 cup dark rum
4 eggs

Glaze
1/4 water
3/4 cup sugar
3/4 cup butter
1/4 cup rum

In a large bowl, combine the cake and pudding mixes together then add oil, water, and rum. Add eggs, one at a time, while stirring. Pour batter into Dutch oven, cover, and bake, using 7 coals underneath the oven and 13 coals on top, for 1 hour. Cool 10 minutes, poke holes in cake, and pour glaze over top. Cool completely and remove from Dutch oven.

GLAZE
In a small saucepan using a bed of coals (about 8–10 coals) or a small camp stove, heat water, sugar, and butter, stirring until sugar dissolves; remove from heat and add rum.

SERVES 12

RHUBARB
BREAD PUDDING

12-inch Dutch oven
11 coals on bottom
17 coals on top
375 degrees

3 eggs
1 cup milk
1/2 teaspoon nutmeg
1/2 teaspoon cinnamon
1/2 cup melted butter
1 1/3 cups sugar
3 1/2 cups cubed bread
4 cups diced rhubarb

Sauce
2 tablespoons butter
2 tablespoons flour
1/2 cup water
1/2 cup bourbon
3/4 cup sugar
1 teaspoon vanilla

In a large bowl, mix eggs, milk, nutmeg, cinnamon, and butter together. Add sugar, bread cubes, and rhubarb to egg mixture. Cover and bake, using 11 coals underneath the oven and 17 coals on top, for 45 minutes. Serve with sauce.

SAUCE

In a small saucepan using a bed of coals (about 8–10 coals) or a small camp stove, melt butter and stir in flour until smooth. Gradually add water, bourbon, sugar, and vanilla. Bring to boil; cook and stir for 2 minutes or until thickened.

SERVES 14–16

CARROT CAKE
EXTRA

2 (10-inch) Dutch ovens
8 coals on bottom of each oven
15 coals on top of each oven
350 degrees

Cake

1 1/2 cups cooking oil
4 eggs
2 teaspoons vanilla
1 1/2 cups sugar
2 cups unbleached flour
1 1/2 teaspoons baking powder
2 teaspoons baking soda
1 teaspoon salt
1 tablespoon cinnamon
1/2 teaspoon nutmeg
2 1/2 cups finely grated carrots
1 cup shredded coconut
1 can (8 ounces) crushed pineapple, drained
1/2 cup finely chopped nuts

Frosting

1/2 cup unsalted butter
8 ounces cream cheese, softened
3 1/2 cups powdered sugar or more as needed

In a medium bowl, beat together oil, eggs, vanilla, and sugar. In a large bowl, blend the flour, baking powder, baking soda, salt, and spices together. Add the liquid ingredients and stir just enough to combine. Gently fold in carrots, coconut, pineapple, and nuts. Equally divide the batter between both Dutch ovens. Cover and bake, using 8 coals underneath the ovens and 15 coals on the tops, for 40–50 minutes. Remove cakes and let cool completely.

FROSTING

In a large bowl, beat together frosting ingredients. Frost cooled cakes.

SERVES 12

RESOURCES

DUTCH OVENS AND SUPPLIES

LODGE
www.lodgemfg.com

CAMP CHEF
www.campchef.com

CAJUN CLASSIC
www.cajuncastiron.com

DUTCH OVEN SOCIETIES

INTERNATIONAL DUTCH OVEN SOCIETY (IDOS)
www.idos.org

LONE STAR DUTCH OVEN SOCIETY (LDOS)
www.lsdos.com

ARKANSAS DUTCH OVEN SOCIETY
www.arkdos.org

ALABAMA DUTCH OVEN SOCIETY
www.alabamadog.com

LOUISIANA DUTCH OVEN SOCIETY
www.ladutch.com

SOUTHERN CALIFORNIA DUTCH OVEN SOCIETY
www.socaldos.org

WESTERN NEW YORK DUTCH OVEN SOCIETY
www.dutchovendave.com

FORTUNA DUTCH OVEN SOCIETY
www.fortunadutchoven.com

LAS VEGAS DOS
www.dosn.org

CENTRAL OKLAHOMA DOS
www.codos.us

LITTLE HOUSE COOKERS DOS
www.lhcmn.com

BAYOUPOTS
www.bayoupots.org

HEARTLAND OF THE PRAIRIE
www.heartlandoftheprairie.org

Be sure to do an internet search as these sites might change and new sites may have been added. There are also a growing number of sites being added to Facebook. In addition, you might also search for NDOGs or National Dutch Oven Gatherings that might be happening in your area.

INDEX

BILL RYAN retired from the United States Air Force in 2002 after serving for 21 years. He now works as a civilian employee and continues to serve his country. He met his wife while he was stationed in Louisiana and decided to call the state home.

He is the president and founder of the Louisiana Dutch Oven Society and serves on the board of directors of the International Dutch Oven Society as the representative for the southern states region. He started cooking with Dutch ovens as a hobby in 2000, has participated in Dutch oven cook-offs since 2007, and enjoys teaching others about cooking in Dutch ovens. He lives with his family in Bossier City, Louisiana.

METRIC CONVERSION CHART

Volume Measurements		Weight Measurements		Temperature Conversion	
U.S.	Metric	U.S.	Metric	Fahrenheit	Celsius
1 teaspoon	5 ml	1/2 ounce	15 g	250	120
1 tablespoon	15 ml	1 ounce	30 g	300	150
1/4 cup	60 ml	3 ounces	90 g	325	160
1/3 cup	75 ml	4 ounces	115 g	350	180
1/2 cup	125 ml	8 ounces	225 g	375	190
2/3 cup	150 ml	12 ounces	350 g	400	200
3/4 cup	175 ml	1 pound	450 g	425	220
1 cup	250 ml	2 1/4 pounds	1 kg	450	230